SHĬ HOLMĔS

Four Investigations

Author and Illustrator: CED / **Translation:** Adam Marostica.
This book is a translation of the original *Quatre enquétes de Sherlock Holmes* © Makaka Éditions

Van Ryder Games and Graphic Novel Adventures are Trademarks of Van Ryder Games LLC
ISBN : 978-0-9997698-4-3   Library of Congress Control Number: 2018933573

Published by Van Ryder Games and printed in China by Long Pack

Find printable investigation sheets and other Graphic Novel Adventures at www.vanrydergames.com

Investigation
Sheet

THE CAT OF BAKER STREET
Where was Mrs. Hudson's cat?

THE LIFELINE
Who assassinated Mrs. Yvette?

THE AMNESIAC OF HIGHGATE WOODS
Who is responsible for
the state of John Doe?

THE SCARAB OF THE BRITISH MUSEUM
Who stole the scarab?

Number of Typewriter keys found :

1.

London

B
S.HOLMES

NO?

WHAT
DO YOU MEAN,
"NO"?

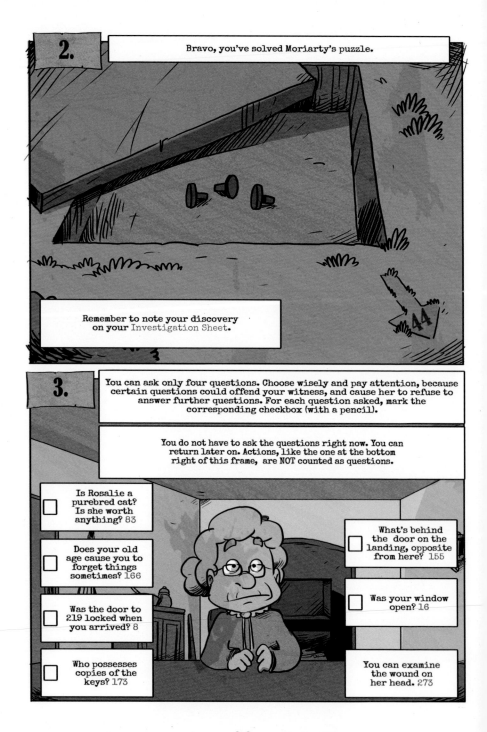

2.

Bravo, you've solved Moriarty's puzzle.

Remember to note your discovery on your Investigation Sheet.

44

3.

You can ask only four questions. Choose wisely and pay attention, because certain questions could offend your witness, and cause her to refuse to answer further questions. For each question asked, mark the corresponding checkbox (with a pencil).

You do not have to ask the questions right now. You can return later on. Actions, like the one at the bottom right of this frame, are NOT counted as questions.

Is Rosalie a purebred cat? Is she worth anything? 83

Does your old age cause you to forget things sometimes? 166

Was the door to 219 locked when you arrived? 8

Who possesses copies of the keys? 173

What's behind the door on the landing, opposite from here? 155

Was your window open? 16

You can examine the wound on her head. 273

6.

THERE WERE ONLY FOUR OF US PREPARING THE EXHIBITION. ARCHAE-OLOGIST: SARAH ANN FORBES, SECURITY GUARD: EMIL JACKSON, MY ASSISTANT: MAUD FORRESTER, AND MYSELF.

Return to 152.

7.

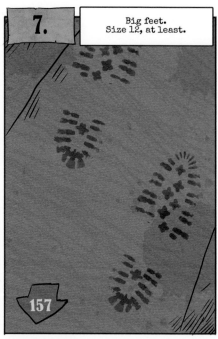

Big feet.
Size 12, at least.

157

8.

YES. IT WAS LOCKED. AND I MADE SURE TO CLOSE IT BEHIND ME. IF NOT, I WOULD HAVE TOLD YOU.

Return to 3.

9.

If this is the first time you've seen this vagabond, go to 104.

Otherwise, go to 153.

Return to 170.

13.

INDEED, I HAVE SEEN THIS MAN. I HID IT FROM YOU BECAUSE I DIDN'T WANT ANY TROUBLE.

AS YOU KNOW, I CAME HERE NOT LONG AGO. THE CITY HAD JUST ASSIGNED ME TO THE CEMETERY. THAT DAY, I WENT THERE TO SEE IF EVERYTHING WAS IN ORDER.

WHEN I WALKED BY THE SHED, IT LOOKED AS THOUGH SOMETHING WAS MOVING INSIDE.

?

I COULD BARELY SEE, BUT... I WAS CERTAIN I SAW A MAN TIED TO A CHAIR.

?

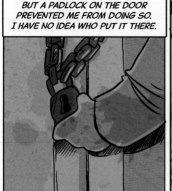

I WANTED TO RESCUE HIM, BUT A PADLOCK ON THE DOOR PREVENTED ME FROM DOING SO. I HAVE NO IDEA WHO PUT IT THERE.

I WENT HOME TO GRAB MY BOLT CUTTERS, AND RETURNED TO THE CEMETERY.

WHEN I ARRIVED, I SAW THAT POOR SOUL. IF ONLY YOU COULD'VE SEEN HIM...

...BUT THE MAN WAS NOT DEAD! I UNTIED HIM. THE KNOTS WERE WELL TIED. I ENDED UP HAVING TO USE MY BOLT CUTTERS ON THEM.

I CARRIED HIM TO A RESIDENTIAL ROAD, AND LEFT HIM THERE. I KNEW THAT ONCE HE WOKE, HE WOULD BE ABLE TO FIND HIS OWN WAY.

BUT WHY NOT INFORM THE AUTHORITIES? OR TAKE HIM TO A POLICE STATION?

I KNOW THAT'S WHAT I SHOULD HAVE DONE, BUT THE MAN WAS IN MY SHED. I'VE HAD RUN-INS WITH THE LAW BEFORE. I DIDN'T WANT TO BE ACCUSED OF ANYTHING.

I SEE...

NOW YOU KNOW THE WHOLE STORY.

Is Garrett Norwood, the grave digger, telling the truth?

Return to 246.

14.

307

Noted by John Watson:

The British Museum stood proudly in front of us, massive and intimidating. Holmes walked with a determined pace, glancing at me with a look of urgency.

The message was clear: We must hurry, for the case awaiting us was making him quiver with impatience.

15.

Cemetery

44

16.

YES, BUT IT HAS BARS ON IT, AS YOU CAN SEE. SPECIFICALLY TO KEEP ROSALIE FROM ESCAPING.

Return to 3.

17.

4

18.

THERE WAS THE GOLD DIGGER, AND THE FROBISHERS. OH, AND A VAGABOND WAS HANGING AROUND THE CEMETERY, IT SEEMS.

Return to 246.

19.

NOTHING TO REPORT! NO ONE IN OR OUT!

209

20.

IF YOU COULD TELL US WHAT HAPPENED AT THE TIME OF THE THEFT, MISTER...

ATKINSON! SAGAMORE ATKINSON!

WHAT HAPPENED...

THE END OF MY CAREER, THAT'S WHAT HAPPENED.

THE MUSEUM HAD BEEN CLOSED TO THE PUBLIC. IN THE EARLY AFTERNOON, I WELCOMED MISS FORBES, ONE OF THE ARCHAEOLOGISTS WORKING FOR OUR MUSEUM. SHE'D COME TO DELIVER THE RELIC.

PROCEDURE DICTATES THAT MISS FORBES MUST ASSURE THAT THE DELIVERY ARRIVES SAFELY IN MY OFFICE. SO, SHE STAYED WITH US.

I MADE SURE OF ITS AUTHENTICITY. OF THAT, I CAN ASSURE YOU.

ONE THING IS CERTAIN. THE SCARAB I PLACED IN THE CASE WAS THE REAL ONE. MISS FORBES CAN ATTEST TO THAT.

Go to 152.

21.

From now on, we will call this fingerprint the GREEN DOCUMENT.
And are you going to show it to agent Bradstreet?

↙ 136

22.

YES, SARAH ANN SENT A COURIER TO EXPLAIN WHY THE FAKE WAS MADE. I DON'T KNOW HOW IT ENDED UP THERE.

Return to 61.

23.

DOCTOR...

...I DON'T WANT TO TELL YOU WHAT SHOULD BE OBVIOUS, BUT A HAMMER WOULD NEVER LEAVE SUCH A SCAR!

You are not a keen observer! Go to 162 to decide how to proceed.

24.

Noted by Sherlock Holmes:
The wound was thin and straight, delivered
with one blow. But what was the murder weapon?

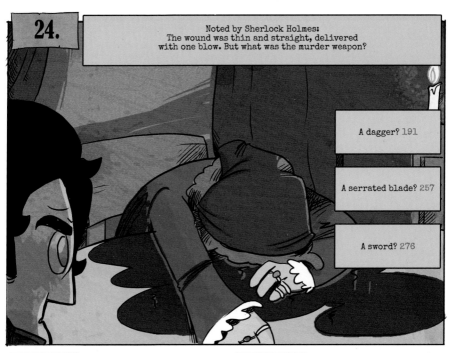

A dagger? 191

A serrated blade? 257

A sword? 276

25.

Noted by Sherlock Holmes:
No... I was not
there at all...

Never mind, return to 297 and cease
using your powers of deduction
in regards to John Doe.

26.

IT LOOKS VAGUELY LIKE A MAP OF THE WOODS. BUT EVEN THOUGH I KNOW THEM WELL, IT DOESN'T MAKE SENSE TO ME...

Return to 153.

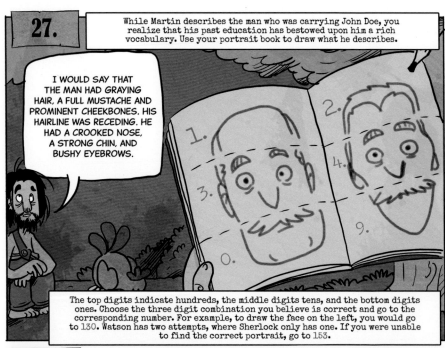

27.

While Martin describes the man who was carrying John Doe, you realize that his past education has bestowed upon him a rich vocabulary. Use your portrait book to draw what he describes.

I WOULD SAY THAT THE MAN HAD GRAYING HAIR, A FULL MUSTACHE AND PROMINENT CHEEKBONES. HIS HAIRLINE WAS RECEDING. HE HAD A CROOKED NOSE, A STRONG CHIN, AND BUSHY EYEBROWS.

1. 2. 3. 4. 9. 0.

The top digits indicate hundreds, the middle digits tens, and the bottom digits ones. Choose the three digit combination you believe is correct and go to the corresponding number. For example, to draw the face on the left, you would go to 130. Watson has two attempts, where Sherlock only has one. If you were unable to find the correct portrait, go to 153.

28.

85

187

29.

NOT REALLY. SOMEONE OFFERED IT TO HIM, BUT WHEN I DISCOVERED IT, I ORDERED HIM TO RETURN IT.

Return to 116.

30.

48

31.

NO, IT IS NOT A REGISTER STRICTLY SPEAKING, BUT THERE IS A NUMEROLOGY NOTEBOOK. THE FIRST THING THAT CLIENTS DO DURING A SEANCE IS TO WRITE THEIR NAME. MADAME YVETTE MAKES HER PREDICTIONS BASED ON THEIR WRITING, AS WELL AS THE NUMBER OF LETTERS IN THEIR FIRST AND LAST NAME.

Return to 68.

32.

Noted by Sherlock Holmes: No... I was not there at all...

Never mind, return to 247 and cease using your powers of deduction in regards to the footprints.

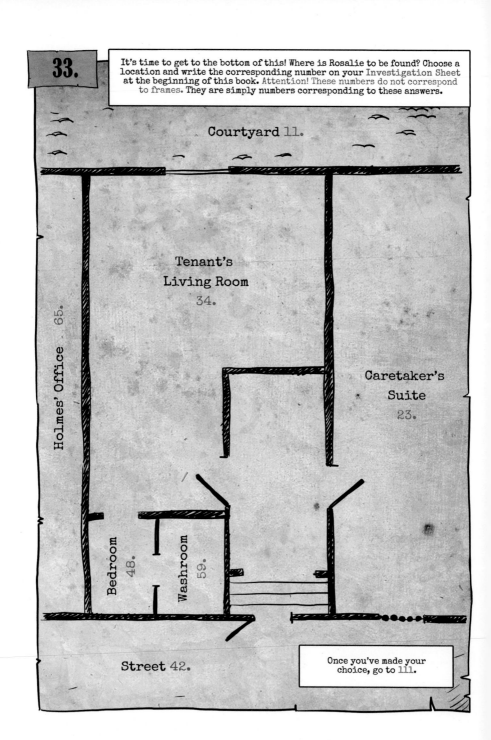

33.

It's time to get to the bottom of this! Where is Rosalie to be found? Choose a location and write the corresponding number on your Investigation Sheet at the beginning of this book. Attention! These numbers do not correspond to frames. They are simply numbers corresponding to these answers.

Courtyard 11.

Tenant's Living Room 34.

Holmes' Office 65.

Caretaker's Suite 23.

Bedroom 48.

Washroom 59.

Street 42.

Once you've made your choice, go to 111.

34. You find a handkerchief in the trash. There's a blood stain: the killer must have used it to clean their weapon, then thrown it away. It is good quality fabric.

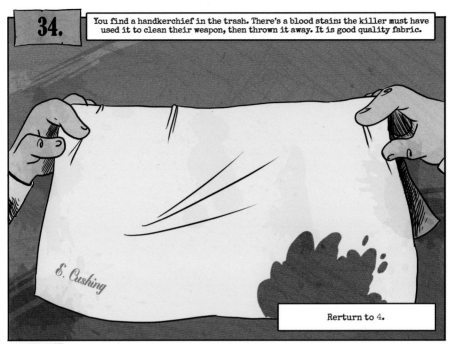

Rerturn to 4.

35.

36.

TELL US YOUR VERSION OF THE FACTS.

I'LL TRY MY BEST.

WE CLOSED THE MUSEUM WHILE WE WAITED FOR THE GOLDEN SCARAB TO BE DELIVERED.

IT WAS A GOOD OPPORTUNITY FOR ME TO CHAT WITH SARAH ANN, WHO I QUITE LIKE.

FROM THE OFFICE, I HEARD THE CURATOR CALL FOR ME. HE WANTED ME TO HELP HIM CLOSE THE WINDOWS IN THE SARCOPHAGUS ROOM, AS A STORM WAS APPROACHING.

I PASSED BY THE SCARAB ON MY WAY AND EVERYTHING SEEMED NORMAL.

JUST AS I TURNED TO HEAD FOR THE WEST WING, I HEARD GLASS CRASHING.

WHEN I ARRIVED AT THE SOURCE OF THE SOUND, THE CASE HAD BEEN BROKEN AND... THE SCARAB WAS GONE!

I RAN UP THE STAIRS TO THE OFFICE AS QUICKLY AS I COULD IN SEARCH OF THE CURATOR.

I COULDN'T FIND HIM, SO I HEADED BACK DOWN. I SAW EMIL, AND THERE... THE SCARAB HAD RETURNED!

EVERYONE WAS TRULY SHOCKED WHEN SARAH ANN CONFIRMED THAT THIS SCARAB WAS A FAKE.

WE HAVE A FEW OTHER QUESTIONS TO ASK YOU.

Ask questions of Miss Forester in 61.

37.

It's time to get to the bottom of this! Who killed Madame Yvette? Choose a person and write the corresponding number on your Investigation Sheet, at the beginning of this book. Heads up! These numbers do not correspond to frames! They are simply numbers corresponding to these answers.

Duke
Benedict Brighton
26.

The Duke's son,
Jeremiah Brighton
58.

The Duke's servant,
John Walter
15.

Madame Yvette's
assistant, Julie
38.

A Client,
Stephen Husk
49.

Mordecai
Cushing
67.

Once you've made your
choice, go to 50.

38.

THE CLIENT ARRIVED AND WROTE HIS NAME IN THE NUMEROLOGY NOTEBOOK. MADAME YVETTE ANALYSED IT, AND ASKED SEVERAL QUESTIONS. THEN SHE READ THE CLIENT'S FUTURE BY LOOKING AT THE PALM OF HIS HAND. FINALLY, HE LEFT AND THE NEXT PERSON TOOK HIS PLACE.

Return to 68.

39.

You have come here to investigate "The Amnesiac of Highgate Woods".

If this is not true, return to the index at 170.

40.

NOTHING TO REPORT. MISS FORRESTER HASN'T MOVED, AND NO ONE HAS COME.

315

41.

Well done! Remember to make note of your work on your Investigation Sheet, at the beginning of the book.

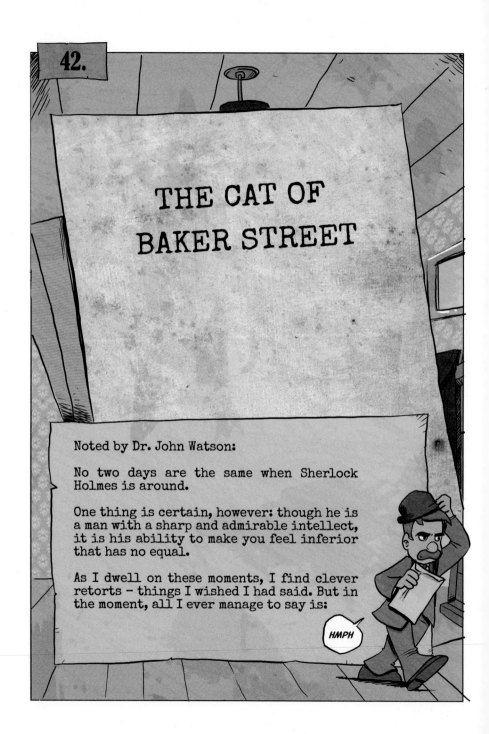

42.

THE CAT OF BAKER STREET

Noted by Dr. John Watson:

No two days are the same when Sherlock Holmes is around.

One thing is certain, however: though he is a man with a sharp and admirable intellect, it is his ability to make you feel inferior that has no equal.

As I dwell on these moments, I find clever retorts – things I wished I had said. But in the moment, all I ever manage to say is:

HMPH

AND CLOSE THE DOOR, I NEED SILENCE IN ORDER TO CONCENTRATE.

AS YOU WISH, HOLMES!

He had entrusted me with cases in the past, but each time hiding some important detail: a gambit to better trap the criminal, if our Baskerville investigation is any indication.

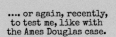

.... or again, recently, to test me, like with the Ames Douglas case.

But this was no time for resentment: I had an investigation to conduct.

Even though this case seemed of minor importance, I would investigate it to the best of my ability, all the same.

LET'S START WITH THE ADDRESS.

HOLMES SAID IT WAS NEARBY.

BAKER STREET

OH !

In this instance, he did not mislead me.

219

43.

Noted by Sherlock Holmes:

The idea that we were heading into a trap kept haunting me. After all, the person who put me on this trail was none other than Professor Moriarty, the most genius criminal I've ever encountered.

But, my preliminary investigations confirmed the lead: it was indeed a very real case. The fact that Inspector Lestrade was standing in front of the door also helped confirm we were onto something.

44.

You have come here to investigate "The Amnesiac of Highgate Woods". If this is not true, return to the index at 170.

When you are finished, go to 58.

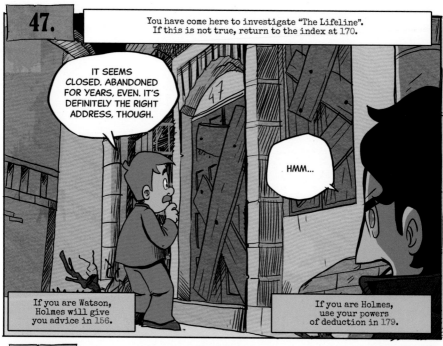

Note that you found a typewriter key on your Investigation Sheet, at the beginning of the book. Take note, if you return to a frame you have already visited, you may not collect a key you have previously found.

BUT THAT'S NOT ALL, THERE IS ALSO A DOCUMENT THAT MORIARTY CALLS THE "INDEX".

HE ASSEMBLED THE ADDRESSES OF ALL THE LOCATIONS AND PERSONS OF INTEREST PERTINENT TO OUR INVESTIGATIONS.

You can find the index at 170.

SO, WATSON, WHICH INVESTIGATION WOULD YOU LIKE TO START WITH?

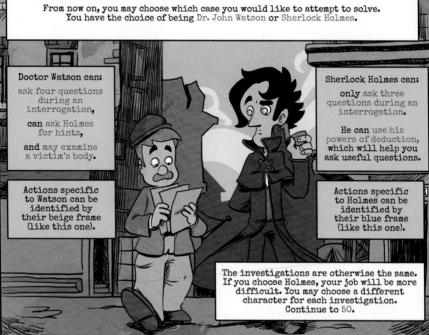

From now on, you may choose which case you would like to attempt to solve. You have the choice of being Dr. John Watson or Sherlock Holmes.

Doctor Watson can:

ask four questions during an interrogation,

can ask Holmes for hints,

and may examine a victim's body.

Actions specific to Watson can be identified by their beige frame (like this one).

Sherlock Holmes can:

only ask three questions during an interrogation.

He can use his powers of deduction, which will help you ask useful questions.

Actions specific to Holmes can be identified by their blue frame (like this one).

The investigations are otherwise the same. If you choose Holmes, your job will be more difficult. You may choose a different character for each investigation.
Continue to 50.

Now, you must choose which investigation
to begin, and as which character!

THE LIFELINE

As Holmes : 43

As Watson : 127

THE AMNESIAC OF
HIGHGATE WOODS

As Holmes : 124

As Watson : 142

THE SCARAB OF
THE BRITISH MUSEUM

As Holmes : 102

As Watson : 14

Once you have completed the three
investigations, go to 317.

51.

NEVER SEEN HIM IN MY LIFE.

Return to 246.

52.

COUNTERFEITS ARE COMMONLY MADE TO AVOID THEFT DURING LONG JOURNEYS. I SENT A NOTE TO THE MUSEUM TO WARN THEM, BUT I'M NOT SURE IF THEY RECEIVED IT.

Return to 306.

53.

What next?

Return to the British Museum? 75

Consult the index? 170

Solve the case! 60

54.

IT'S RATHER SIMPLE! IF THE DAGGER WERE DIRTY, IT'S BECAUSE NO ONE HAD TAKEN THE EFFORT TO CLEAN IT. IF IT HAD BEEN USED TO KILL SOMEONE, THERE WOULD ALSO BE TRACES OF BLOOD. THEREFORE, IT IS NOT THE WEAPON WE'RE LOOKING FOR.

Return to 93.

55.

This path leads to the street. The assassin must have fled down the alley.

4

56.

No good! If you have any tries left, go to 294. Otherwise, go to 53. You may not return to Emil Jackson.

57.

HE ARRIVED A FEW DAYS AGO. HE DIDN'T COME FROM LONDON. MY UNDERSTANDING IS THAT HE'S HERE LOOKING FOR SOMETHING. THAT'S ALL I KNOW.

Return to 153.

58.

What now?

Return to the police station to see John Doe. 297

Return to the cemetery. 44

Consult the GREY PAPER (if you've found it). 92

Consult the index. 170

I've done it. I've solved the case! 74

MAY I PLEASE SEE YOUR BARE TORSO? I'D LIKE TO EXAMINE YOU.

SURE.

Noted by John Watson: Poor chap! Even in all my years of medicine, rarely have I seen such cruel injuries.

Among others, I noted missing teeth...

bruises, wounds, and burns on his arms and torso...

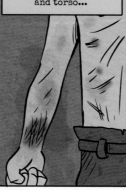

and cuts on his wrists that indicate that he had been tied up.

YOU CAN PUT THIS BACK ON. THE DOCTOR TOOK GOOD CARE OF YOU.

There was no doubt in my mind. This man had been immobilized and tortured. It was certainly this trauma that caused his amnesia.

Return to 297.

60.

It's time to get to the bottom of this! According to you, who stole the scarab? Choose a person and write the corresponding number on your Investigation Sheet, at the beginning of this book. Attention! These numbers do not correspond to frames. They are simply numbers corresponding to these answers.

The Curator,
Sagamore Atkinson
23.

The Assistant,
Maud Forrester
57.

The Archaeologist,
Sarah Ann Forbes
39.

The Security Guard,
Emil Jackson
46.

Once you've made your choice, go to 50.

61.

If you are Watson, you may ask four questions, but only three if you are Holmes. For each question asked, mark the corresponding checkbox (with a pencil). Be careful, as certain questions could offend your witness, and cause them to refuse to answer further questions.

☐ Were you aware of the existence of a counterfeit? 22

☐ Would you say you are well paid here? 112

☐ Where did you go, exactly, to secure the relics during the storm? 208

☐ How do you get along with your team? 268

☐ Who does the hammer belong to? 243

☐ How much would the relic go for on the market? 223

If you've found it, show her the PINK ENVELOPE. 125

When you are done, go to 53. You may return.

62.

You have come here to investigate "The Scarab of the British Museum". If this is not true, return to the index at 170.

209

19

63.

The security guard's booth.

→ **75**

64.

WE SAW HIM COME THIS WAY A COUPLE DAYS BACK. HE CAME TO TALK TO US, AS HE DID WITH THE REST OF THE NEIGHBORHOOD.

Return to 293.

65.

SHE'S UPSTAIRS, BUT CAN'T SEE ANYONE. SHE'S NOT FEELING WELL.

Return to 116.

66.

WHO IS IT?! *LEAVE US ALONE!*

GET OFF MY PROPERTY OR I WILL PULL THIS TRIGGER, I PROMISE YOU!

What a welcome! If you found the handkerchief, go to 213. Otherwise, return to the scene of the crime at 172 or the index at 170.

I STAYED A FEW MINUTES TO KEEP HER COMPANY, THEN I FILLED HER FOOD AND WATER BOWLS. WHILE I DID SO, ROSALIE WALKED OUT INTO THE HALL.

BUT WHILE I WAS BENDING DOWN...

...SOMETHING HIT ME HARD ON THE BACK OF MY HEAD.

I HEARD SEVERAL IDENTICAL BUT MUTED SOUNDS, THEN...

...NOTHING!

I DON'T KNOW HOW LONG I WAS OUT FOR.

...

WHEN I REGAINED CONSCIOUSNESS, I WAS LAYING ON THE FLOOR.

ROSALIE WAS GONE! I LOOKED FOR HER HERE IN THE CARETAKER'S SUITE, IN THE HALL (THAT STAYED CLOSED), I CALLED OUT HER NAME...

...NO TRACE OF HER ANYWHERE!

HMM... QUITE STRANGE! MAY I ASK YOU A FEW QUESTIONS?

ASK ME ANYTHING YOU LIKE, IF YOU THINK IT WILL HELP YOU FIND MY ROSALIE!

It's up to you! Ask Mrs. Hudson the right questions at 3.

68.

If you are Watson, you may ask four questions, but only three if you are Holmes. For each question asked, mark the corresponding checkbox (with a pencil). Be careful, as certain questions could offend your witness, and cause them to refuse to answer further questions.

☐ Who yelled? And what did they yell? 182

☐ Does Madame Yvette truly have a gift? 200

☐ Do you have a registry of the clientele? 31

☐ Why didn't she predict her own death? 81

☐ What did the seances consist of? 38

☐ Did she have any enemies? 274

When you are done, return to 172.

69.

Noted by Sherlock Holmes: This deduction was simply ridiculous. This is not one my finer moments...

Nevermind, return to 247 and cease using your powers of deduction in regards to the footprints.

70.

I GET ALONG WELL WITH EVERYONE. IT'S JUST WITH MY ASSISTANT, MISS FORESTER, THAT THINGS ARE A LITTLE... COMPLICATED. SHE... LIKES ME, FOR REASONS I COULDN'T POSSIBLY UNDERSTAND.

Return to 152.

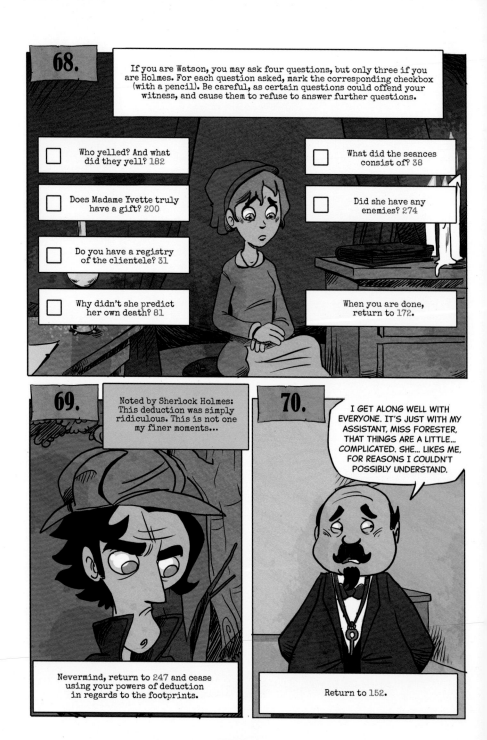

71.

You have come here to investigate "The Scarab of the British Museum". If this is not true, return to the index at 170.

72.

Noted by Sherlock Holmes: No, that's not it. There's a more simple explanation, I'm sure of it.

Nevermind, return to 136 and cease using your powers of deduction in regards to the fingerprints.

73.

NO IDEA WHAT THAT'S SUPPOSED TO BE.

Return to 293.

74.

It's time to get to the bottom of this! Who is responsible for John Doe's condition? Choose a person and write the corresponding number on your Investigation Sheet, at the beginning of this book. Attention! These numbers do not correspond to frames. They are simply numbers corresponding to these answers.

The Amnesiac,
John Doe
10.

The Gravedigger,
Garrett Norwood
54.

The Vagabond,
Martin Norris
35.

The Gold Digger,
Horace Owen
44.

Morris Frobisher,
Retired
62.

Edna Frobisher,
Retired
78.

Once you've made your choice, go to 50.

76.

You find a love letter. From now on, we call this document, THE PINK ENVELOPE.

My dear Emil,
Do you remember the old days, when we were happy?
Working with Atkinson eats away at me a little more every day!
I promise, once this exhibition is finished, we will go far away, just like we said we would!
Your love.

Go to 53. You may not return to Emil Jackson.

77.

Now upstairs, you step into the office that the curator and his assistant share.

S. Atkinson

272

216

M. Forrester

313

75

78.

ONE NIGHT, I SAW A MAN LEAVE THE CEMETERY CARRYING YOUR STRANGER ON HIS SHOULDERS. WOULD YOU LIKE ME TO DESCRIBE THE MAN TO YOU?

Go to 27.

79.

Nothing to see here.

80.

Jonathan Brighton's dagger is missing. Only the sheath remains.

Return to 181.

81.

DO YOU THINK YOU'RE CLEVER ASKING QUESTIONS LIKE THAT? DO YOU REALLY THINK THAT THIS IS AN APPROPRIATE TIME TO BE MAKING JOKES?

Uh-oh! Julie is offended and will not answer any more of your questions! You may not return to see her again. Return to 172.

82.

YES, MY FATHER FORCED ME TO GO SOMETIMES. FOR SOME TIME NOW.

Return to 181.

83.

NO, ROSALIE ISN'T WORTH ANYTHING, BESIDES SENTIMENTAL VALUE, OF COURSE.

Return to 3.

84.

I BARELY LOOKED, BUT IT SEEMED THAT SHE WAS PREGNANT.

Return to 128.

85.

Vacation

request

John Walter

Return to 187.

86.

253

157 →

232

266

↘ **44**

87.

There's no one inside.

↓ **288**

88.

YES... WELL, NO! I MEAN, I AM A CIVILIZED MAN. THAT'S NOT THE REASON I LIVE FAR FROM OTHER... UH...

You've frightened Martin. You may not ask him any further questions. Return to 153.

89.

THAT I DO NOT KNOW! I'M NOT FAMILIAR WITH THE METHODS OF COUNTERFEITING!

Return to 152.

90.

HE IS NO LONGER THERE, BUT HE WAS!

LOOK, HE DROPPED SOMETHING!

76

91.

YEAH, THAT'S HIM!

Return to 153.

It looks like a map. You notice that
there's something written on the back...

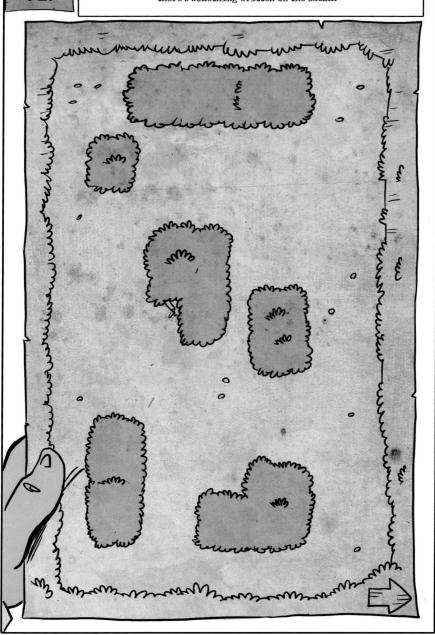

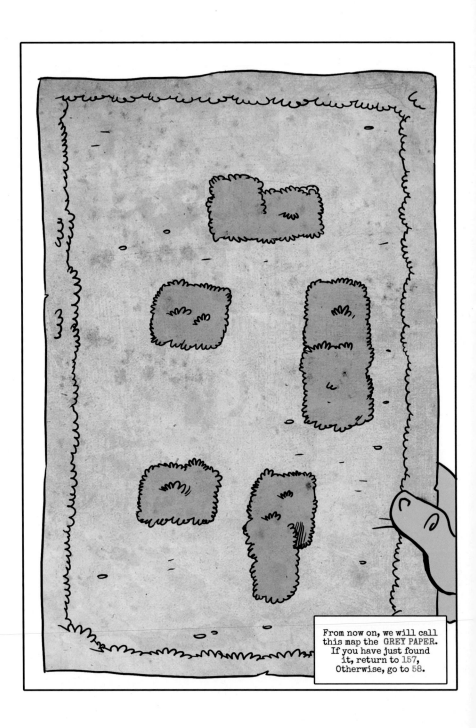

From now on, we will call
this map the GREY PAPER.
If you have just found
it, return to 157,
Otherwise, go to 58.

93.

If you are Watson, you may ask four questions, but only three if you are Holmes. For each question asked, mark the corresponding checkbox (with a pencil). Be careful, as certain questions could offend your witness, and cause them to refuse to answer further questions.

☐ Do you have a dagger? 164

☐ Do you have any reason to be angry with Madame Yvette? 186

☐ Why did you consult her regarding your son? 262

☐ Do you believe in her powers? 174

☐ Was there anyone in her waiting room when you left? 280

☐ Why didn't you want to sign your real name? 285

When you're finished, go to 311.

94.

247

300

96.

Noted by John Watson: The room was quite small, perfect for a bachelor.

97.

Husk has become upset. Return to 128, but you may not ask him any more questions.

98.

Noted by Sherlock Holmes: No... That wasn't the answer I was looking for. But all things considered, it got me thinking.

Return to 93.

99.

A piece of paper! It must have fallen and become stuck between the floorboards.

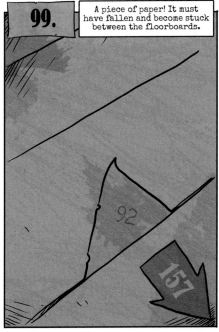

102.

Noted by Sherlock Holmes:

As we arrived at the British Museum, I noticed something unusual. The courtyard is usually a noisy place, teeming with an excited crowd eager for knowledge, but now... it was deserted. No other clues were needed. Something happened here, and we were going to get to the bottom of it.

103.

You have come here to investigate "The Amnesiac of Highgate Woods". If this is not true, return to the index at 170. Otherwise, the Frobishers would be happy to answer your questions at 293.

153

105.

4

172

106.

I ARRIVED A SHORT TIME AGO, BUT EVERYONE TALKS OF A TREASURE... EVEN IF THEY'VE NEVER SEEN A MAP.

Return to 246.

107.

YOU MEAN, ASIDE FROM IT'S PRICELESS HISTORICAL VALUE? MILLIONS, IF YOU KNOW THE RIGHT BUYER.

Return to 152.

108.

No one answers when you knock! But... the door is open!

314

109.

You recognize the signature and the writing: it's a puzzle left by Moriarty, to test you! If you don't know how to solve it, don't worry. It won't affect the current investigation.

110.

You notice that the hammer is missing from Miss Forbes' tools. The others look covered with prints.

111.

MRS. HUDSON! I THINK I KNOW WHERE TO FIND ROSALIE! LOOK, I MARKED IT ON THE MAP. IF THE TWO US *GO* TO VERIF--

WATSON! QUIT AMUSING YOURSELF AND FOLLOW ME!

I *NEED* YOU!

HOLMES? BUT I WAS JUST ABOUT TO TAKE MRS. HUDSON TO HER CAT!

OUR LANDLORD HAS LEGS! SHE CAN TAKE HERSELF THERE. COME, THIS IS URGENT!

Don't worry, you will complete this first investigation later on at the end of your adventure... For now, follow Holmes to 49.

112.

QUITE BADLY, AS A MATTER OF FACT... BUT THAT QUESTION SEEMS AWFULLY PERSONAL.

You seem to have upset Miss Forrester. Return to 61, but you may not ask her any more questions.

113.

Noted by Sherlock Holmes: Voila! The person who broke the case wore gloves. Then another person, with bare hands, placed the fake scarab.

Return to 136.

114.

THIS DOESN'T CHANGE ANYTHING! IT WASN'T THAT!

If you have any attempts remaining, return to 210, Otherwise, go to 35.

115.

Closed! And no one is answering.

Retrace your steps to 219.

116.

If you are Watson, you may ask four questions, but only three if you are Holmes. For each question asked, mark the corresponding checkbox (with a pencil). Be careful, as certain questions could offend your witness, and cause him to refuse to answer further questions.

☐ So, it's your daughter's handkerchief? 29

☐ Can we see your daughter? Is she here? 65

☐ Is your daughter seeing anyone? 148

☐ May we inspect Esther's affairs? 195

☐ You mentioned a Duke? 159

☐ Have you been to see Madame Yvette? 175

When you're finished, go to 289.

117.

The numerology notebook: clients write their first and last name, and Madame Yvette makes predictions based on the number of letters in their name. This is the page corresponding to the day of the crime. We recommend placing a bookmark here, so that you can come back and consult this notebook whenever you like. Feel free to compare it with the index on 170.

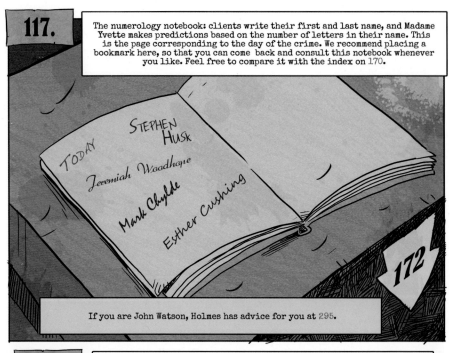

TODAY
STEPHEN HUSK
Jeremiah Woodhope
Mark Chylde
Esther Cushing

172

If you are John Watson, Holmes has advice for you at 295.

118.

It seems that Moriarty has left a puzzle to test you! If you don't know how to solve it, don't worry. It won't affect the current investigation.

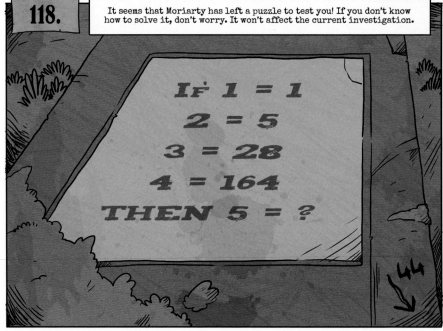

If 1 = 1
2 = 5
3 = 28
4 = 164
THEN 5 = ?

44

119.

The case was closed. You notice that the lock is still intact and doesn't seem to have been forced, in any way.

136

120.

I TRUST NO ONE BUT MYSELF. THE KEY HANGS FROM MY NECK, AS YOU CAN SEE.

Return to 152.

121.

You have come here to investigate "The Scarab of the British Museum". If this is not true, return to the index at 170.

315

40

Return to 246.

Noted by Sherlock Holmes:

The first thing that struck me as we approached Highgate was the lugubrious look on my dear friend Dr. Watson's face.

Obviously, far from downtown, the ambience didn't quite enchant him. I informed agent Gregson that we were investigating the case, and that we would soon be joining him at the police station.

125.

AND WILL YOU REVEAL THE TRUTH ABOUT THIS LETTER, MISS FORRESTER?

OH, YOU FOUND THAT...

I SUPPOSE I OWE YOU THE TRUTH...

EMIL AND I.... ARE LOVERS, FOR QUITE SOME TIME NOW. BUT MR. ATKINSON, THE CURATOR, HE HAS ME BY THE NOSE. HE HATES ME, AND NEVER HESITATES TO MAKE SURE THAT I KNOW IT. EMIL AND I MADE THE DECISION TO QUIT THE MUSEUM ONCE THE SCARAB EXHIBITION WAS FINISHED.

WHY DID HE LEAVE HOME?

HE LEFT?

I PROMISE I DON'T KNOW WHERE HE'S GONE--

I'M HERE, MAUD.

AS MAUD SAID, WE WERE PLANNING ON LEAVING, BUT WE NEEDED MONEY. SO, I TOOK ADVANTAGE OF THE FACT THAT EVERYONE WAS PREOCCUPIED WITH THE STORM. I SIMPLY WANTED TO REMOVE THE *CASE*, AND REPLACE THE SCARAB WITH THE FAKE. BUT WHEN THE *CASE GOT STUCK*, I PANICKED. I BROKE IT AND TOOK THE SCARAB, BUT I *GOT CONFUSED* AND PUT THE FAKE IN ITS PLACE.

WAS MISS FORRESTER AWARE OF THIS PLAN?

NO, THIS WAS ALL MY IDEA, I PROMISE YOU.

YOU SHOULD BE SURE TO TELL THIS ALL TO THE POLICE.

OFFICER?

EMIL, *NO!!!*

MISS FORRESTER, I PROMISE YOU THAT NO MATTER WHAT HAPPENED, I WILL FIND THE TRUTH.

Return to 61.

126.

At your request, the Duke pulls his dagger from its sheath. You immediately notice that it is quite dirty.

If you are Watson, Holmes will give you advice at 54.

If you are Holmes, use your powers of deduction at 198.

127.

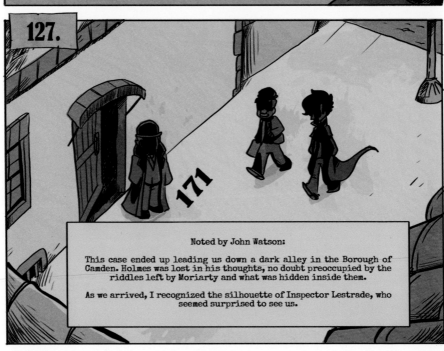

Noted by John Watson:

This case ended up leading us down a dark alley in the Borough of Camden. Holmes was lost in his thoughts, no doubt preoccupied by the riddles left by Moriarty and what was hidden inside them.

As we arrived, I recognized the silhouette of Inspector Lestrade, who seemed surprised to see us.

128.

If you are Watson, you may ask four questions, but only three if you are Holmes. For each question asked, mark the corresponding checkbox (with a pencil). Be careful, as certain questions could offend your witness, and cause him to refuse to answer further questions.

☐ What did she predict for you? 154

☐ How would you describe the man who pushed you? 147

☐ Do you have any sharp weapons? 161

☐ Why did you choose that day to make a complaint? 97

☐ Did the appointments cost you much? 310

☐ Did you notice anything strange about the young woman in the waiting room? 84

When you're finished, you can return to the scene of the crime at 172 or consult the index at 170.

129.

Noted by John Watson: I had arrived at the end of my investigation. It was time to come to a conclusion based on what I had learned and deduced. To start, why did the door slam twice?

Was there a gust of air? 185

Was someone passing very quickly through one door to another? 258

130.

Return to 27. If you're out of attempts, go to 153.

131.

Return to 297.

132.

You notice a dagger under the bed.

133.

Noted by John Watson: My experience as a forensic doctor proved rather useful at the time. I decided to examine the body: the victim was a woman, around 60, killed by a bladed weapon.

A single clean and forceful cut on her left side caused fatal blood loss. A long blade was used or, in all likelihood, a dagger.

The position in which Madame Yvette was found and the location of her injury were both unusual.

Why was her right arm stretched out? Why did the killer stab her in the side, and not the neck or heart?

Then, I understood.

While she was reading their palm, the assassin took the opportunity to pull Madame Yvette by the hand and deliver the fatal blow.

To conclude, I would say that the killer was a client of the fortune teller. Likely a strong, left-handed man.

Return to 172.

134.

YOU MEAN TO POTENTIAL BUYERS? ARE YOU INSINUATING THAT I STOLE IT? IS THIS REALLY HOW YOU WISH TO ADDRESS THE CURATOR OF THE MOST PRESTIGIOUS MUSEUM IN LONDON?

You've offended Atkinson! Return to 152, but ask him no further questions.

135.

THE TIMER CONTINUES TO TURN. THIS ISN'T THE ANSWER!

If you have any remaining attempts, return to 210. Otherwise, go to 35.

136.

You note that the case could not have been broken by hand.

137.

If you are Watson, you can examine the body at 133.

If you are Holmes, use your powers of deduction at 24.

138.

Noted by Sherlock Holmes: No... Something was escaping me, but couldn't put my finger on it.

Return to the scene of the crime at 172 or consult the index at 170.

139.

HE DIDN'T LOOK LIKE THAT.

Return to 27. If you're out of attempts, go to 153.

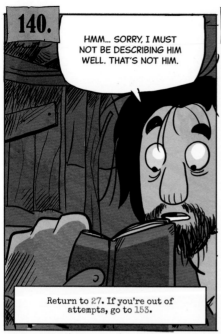

Return to 27. If you're out of attempts, go to 153.

Return to 297.

143.

The dagger is as clean as a newly minted coin. Return to 187.

144.

You have come here to investigate "The Lifeline". If this is not true, return to the index at 170.

The door is shut and no one is answering. Return to the scene of the crime at 172 or to the index at 170.

145.

You have come here to investigate "The Lifeline". If this is not true, return to the index at 170.

THE NUMEROLOGY NOTEBOOK WAS A BIT OF PROBLEM FOR ME, BECAUSE I DIDN'T WISH TO USE MY REAL NAME... MY FAMILY HAS A REPUTATION TO UPHOLD! I HAD TO THINK OF ONE WITH THE SAME NUMBER OF LETTERS.

WHILE I WAS WALKING, I STUMBLED UPON A HOUSE THAT HAD BEEN ABANDONED FOR YEARS. ON THE MAILBOX, A NAME: JEREMIAH WOODHOPE.

IT WAS TOO PERFECT! IT WAS THE SAME NUMBER OF LETTERS, AND I SAW NO RISK IN USING THE NAME, AS THE MAN HAD MOVED AWAY A LONG TIME AGO.

MADAME YVETTE'S LAST PREDICTIONS HAD BEEN PARTICULARLY MACABRE.

A DARK FUTURE IS WRITTEN IN THESE LINES. A BLACK CLOUD APPROACHES.

TROUBLED BY HER WORDS, I LEFT HER OFFICE, LOST IN MY THOUGHTS.

WOULD YOU BE WILLING TO ANSWER A FEW QUESTIONS?

ABSOLUTELY, MY GOOD SIRS.

To begin interrogating Benedict Brighton go to 93.

147.

TALL, I WOULD SAY. I BARELY SAW HIM.

Return to 128.

148.

SHE WAS SEEING SOMEONE, BUT I DIDN'T LIKE IT.

Return to 116.

149.

NO, THAT FACE IS NOT FAMILIAR TO ME.

Return to 27. If you're out of attempts, go to 153.

150.

GENTLEMEN?

If you are visiting the curator for the first time, go to 20. Otherwise, go to 152.

152.

If you are Watson, you may ask four questions, but only three if you are Holmes. For each question asked, mark the corresponding checkbox (with a pencil). Be careful, as certain questions could offend your witness, and cause them to refuse to answer further questions.

☐ What is the scarab worth? 107

☐ Who has the key to the case? 120

☐ Who was in the museum? 6

☐ How do you get along with your team? 70

☐ Would you be rich if you were to resell it? 134

☐ Where did the fake scarab come from? 89

If you've found it, show him the PINK ENVELOPE. 244

When you're finished, go to 75. You may return.

153.

If you are Watson, you may ask four questions, but only three if you are Holmes. For each question asked, mark the corresponding checkbox (with a pencil). Be careful, as certain questions could offend your witness, and cause them to refuse to answer further questions.

☐ Who is that man? 57

☐ Who was he with? 78

☐ What is your shoesize? 226

☐ Does civilization frighten you? 88

☐ Who lives here? 265

☐ Do these woods hold anything special? 279

If you've found it, show him the GREY PAPER. 26

If you've found it, show him the LEATHER NOTEBOOK. 91

When you're finished, go to 58. You can come back later on.

154.

FOR MANY YEARS, SHE HAD PREDICTED A GREAT LOVE WAS IN MY FUTURE.

AND HERE I AM, ALONE WITH MY CATS....

Return to 128.

155.

IT'S THE APARTMENT OF A FUTURE TENANT. HE HAS THE KEYS, BUT THERE'S NO ONE THERE AT THE MOMENT. HE'LL BE MOVING HERE IN A FEW WEEKS.

Return to 3.

156.

THINK, WATSON! WE ARE AT THE ADDRESS OF ONE JEREMIAH WOODHOPE. HOWEVER, THE PLACE HAS BEEN ABANDONED FOR YEARS. IT IS THUS A BORROWED NAME, SO THAT THE REAL PERSON CAN'T BE RECOGNIZED.

BUT, IF THE CLIENT BELIEVES IN MADAME YVETTE'S NUMEROLOGY METHODS, THE PSEUDONYM WILL NO DOUBT HAVE THE SAME NUMBER OF LETTERS AS THE REAL FIRST AND LAST NAME.

Go find him in the index at 170.

157.

To return directly to the cemetery, go to 44.

158.

159.

I DON'T WANT TO TALK ABOUT IT. NO USE GETTING MIXED UP WITH THEM.

Return to 116.

Return to 181.

Return to 128.

163.

You have come here to investigate "The Lifeline".
If this is not true, return to the index at 170.

164.

YES. ALL OF THE MEN IN OUR FAMILY HAVE ONE, WHICH WE ALWAYS CARRY ON OUR BELTS.

Return to 93.

165.

I NEVER PUT A LOCK ON THAT SHED BECAUSE THERE WAS NOTHING THERE WORTH STEALING. AS YOU KNOW, I DON'T VISIT THE CEMETERY OFTEN. NO ONE DOES.

Return to 246.

166.

COME NOW! I'M NOT SO OLD AS THAT! FOR A DOCTOR, YOU HAVE VERY LITTLE TACT!

You've offended Mrs. Hudson. Return to 3, but ask her no further questions.

167.

34

168.

Noted by Sherlock Holmes: No... such a conclusion, as obvious as it seems, doesn't take me anywhere.

Return to 93.

169.

I DON'T KNOW. I DON'T REMEMBER ANYTHING...

Return to 297.

The famous index! Moriarty has assembled the addresses of all the people and places involved in our investigations. It's simple to use it: just go to the frame corresponding to the person or place you're looking for.

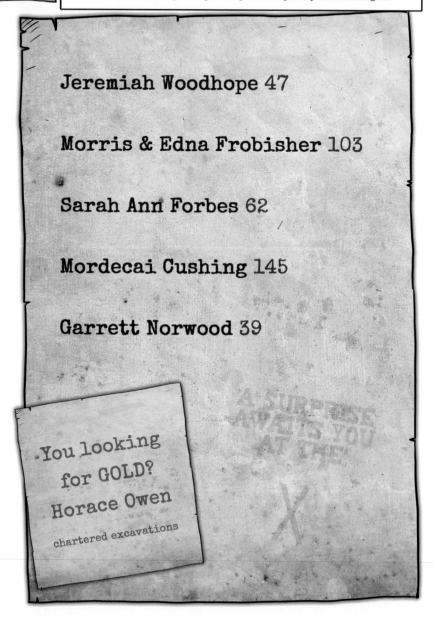

Jeremiah Woodhope 47

Morris & Edna Frobisher 103

Sarah Ann Forbes 62

Mordecai Cushing 145

Garrett Norwood 39

.You looking
for GOLD?
Horace Owen
chartered excavations

A SURPRISE
AWAITS YOU
AT THE

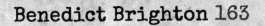

COUNCIL OF CIRTA

Benedict Brighton 163

Horace Owen 288

Maud Forrester 121

Mark Chylde 144

Emil Jackson 71

Highgate
Cemetery 44

Stephen Husk 299

If you are lost, here's a reminder of where you can go.

"The Lifeline", scene of the crime: 172.
"The Amnesiac of Highgate Woods", police station: 297.
"The Scarab of the British Museum", the museum: 75.

171.

HOLMES?! BUT... BUT NO ONE ASKED YOU HERE! AND DON'T GO TELLING ME YOU JUST HAPPENED TO WALK BY THE SCENE OF A MURDER, BECAUSE I'M NOT GOING TO BELIEVE YOU!

ALAS NO, LESTRADE! WE CAUGHT WIND OF A CRIME HERE, AND YOU JUST CONFIRMED FOR ME THAT IT WAS A MURDER. BUT, NOW THAT WE'RE HERE, PERHAPS WE COULD BE OF SOME USE.

AH, TO HECK WITH IT... WHY NOT?

HERE'S THE CASE: WE ARE CURRENTLY OUTSIDE THE FORTUNE TELLING OFFICE OF ONE, MADAME YVETTE. SHE OFFERS CARTOMANCY AND NUMEROLOGY SERVICES TO ALL MANNER OF CLIENTELE, FROM THE RICH TO THE POOR. IT IS TOUGH TO BELIEVE THAT SHE WAS MURDERED RIGHT HERE!

POOR WOMAN, THAT'S AWFUL! WOULD YOU LET US TAKE A QUICK LOOK?

AFTER YOU, GENTLEMEN.

172

172.

Are you sure you've explored everything? Yes? Then go to 289.

173.

THE TENANT OF THE APARTMENT ACROSS THE HALL! HE HAS KEYS TO THE MAIN ENTRANCE AND HIS LODGINGS, BUT NOT THE CARETAKER'S SUITE!

I GAVE THEM TO HIM DURING OUR INTERVIEW, SEVERAL WEEKS AGO, BUT HE WASN'T SUPPOSED TO MOVE IN UNTIL NEXT MONTH.

Return to 3.

174.

I'LL BELIEVE IN WHATEVER I PLEASE, MY FRIEND! YOU HAVE SOME NERVE SPEAKING TO A DUKE LIKE THIS.

You've offended Benedict Brighton. Return to 93, but ask him no further questions.

175.

NO, I DON'T NEED TO SEE A FORTUNE TELLER TO KNOW THAT MISERY IS ALL THE FUTURE HAS IN STORE FOR ME.

Return to 116.

176.

Noted by Sherlock Holmes:

Yes, that's it! Someone brought him here, unconscious, and left him. Then, the amnesiac woke up and wandered off.

Return to 247.

177.

WE'VE CLEARLY GOT SOMETHING WRONG, THE BOMB IS STILL TICKING!

If you have any attempts remaining, return to 210, Otherwise, go to 35.

178.

HMM...

I'M NO DOCTOR, BUT I DON'T BELIEVE SO, NO...

Incorrect! Go to 162 and decide how to proceed.

179.

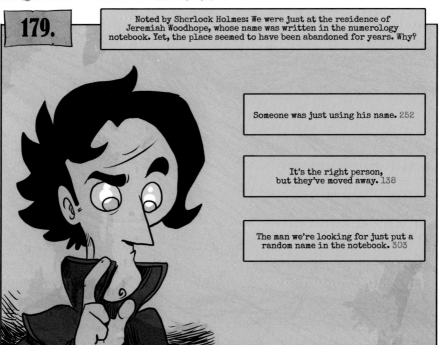

Noted by Sherlock Holmes: We were just at the residence of Jeremiah Woodhope, whose name was written in the numerology notebook. Yet, the place seemed to have been abandoned for years. Why?

Someone was just using his name. 252

It's the right person, but they've moved away. 138

The man we're looking for just put a random name in the notebook. 303

I... UH... I HAD HAD ENOUGH OF HER FALSE PREDICTIONS. NOTHING SHE PREDICTED WAS HAPPENING. BUT... UH... WHY ARE YOU ASKING ME THAT? DO YOU THINK I KILLED HER?

WE SIMPLY DON'T WANT TO MISS ANY DETAILS. PLEASE, GO ON.

HOW DID THE SEANCE END? DID YOU SEE ANYONE IN THE WAITING ROOM WHEN YOU LEFT?

OH, HELLO THERE, KITTY!

THE SEANCE WAS CUT SHORT. SHE REFUSED TO REFUND ME FOR ALL HER YEARS OF SCAMMING. I LEFT FEELING DISGUSTED.

BUT, I DID CROSS PATHS WITH SOMEONE... OR RATHER, SOMEONE BUMPED INTO ME, WITHOUT EVEN EXCUSING THEMSELF.

WE WOULD LIKE TO ASK YOU A FEW QUESTIONS.

IT WON'T TAKE LONG.

To begin interrogating Stephen Husk, go to 128.

181.

If you are Watson, you may ask four questions, but only three if you are Holmes. For each question asked, mark the corresponding checkbox (with a pencil). Be careful, as certain questions could offend your witness, and cause him to refuse to answer further questions.

☐ Have you ever been to see Madame Yvette? 82

☐ Is she good at what she does? 160

☐ Are you seeing anyone right now? 281

☐ May we see your dagger? 302

☐ If you made a big mistake, do you think your father would cover it up? 267

☐ Could you write your name on a scrap of paper? 196

When you're finished, go to 311.

182.

IT WAS MADAME YVETTE I HEARD. SHE SAID: "I PROMISE I WON'T SAY A THING!"

Return to 68.

183.

THE DOOR? YOU THINK THE CORNER OF THE DOOR HIT ME?

MRS. HUDSON, LET ME TRY SOMETHING IN 95.

184.

Behind the curtain we found a tearful young woman. Lestrade introduces you: this is Julie, Madame Yvette's assistant. According to him, she was in this room, right next to that of the crime scene, when it all happened.

GOOD DAY MISS. YOU HAVE OUR CONDOLENCES.

>SNIFF< SORRY... IT'S AWFUL...

COULD YOU TELL US YOUR VERSION OF THE FACTS?

I'VE WORKED FOR MADAME YVETTE FOR SEVERAL YEARS. SHE... SHE ALWAYS TOOK CARE OF ME. I OWE HER EVERYTHING! I WAS JUST HERE, I WAS PREPARING HER ACCESSORIES FOR HER NEXT CLIENT. SHE WAS IN A SEANCE. I... HEARD SCREAMING! I WAS PARALYZED! I RECOVERED AND DARED TO RAISE THE CURTAIN. WHEN I ARRIVED, MADAME YVETTE WAS ALREADY... SHE WAS ALREADY... SHE WAS... SHE...

WE WOULD LIKE TO ASK YOU A FEW QUESTIONS, IF THAT WOULD BE ALRIGHT.

GO AHEAD. >SNIFF<

To interrogate Julie, go to 68.

185.

That's it! I was on the right track! And if it was a gust of wind, it was because...

Two windows were open.
251

Mrs. Hudson caught a cold.
269

186.

NO, SHE WAS ALWAYS GREAT COUNCIL. I HAD NO ISSUE WITH HER.

Return to 93.

187.

28

132

When you're finished, return to 311.

193.

DOES THIS MAP JOG YOUR MEMORY?

IT'S... IT'S WEIRD...

BUT YES! I'M CERTAIN THIS IS MINE.

I GET THE FEELING THAT I CAME TO THESE PARTS BECAUSE OF THIS MAP. I FOUND IT BY ACCIDENT, IN A PLACE FULL OF BOOKS. A LIBRARY! I FOUND IT STUCK IN A BOOK AND IT SAID... DANG, THAT'S ALL I CAN REMEMBER.

NOTHING ELSE COMES TO MIND? SOMETHING THAT WOULD HELP US DECODE IT?

THE WORD "TRANSPARENCY".

?

Return to 297.

194.

LOOKS ENOUGH LIKE MR. NORWOOD, THE NEW GRAVE DIGGER?

DID HE DO SOMETHING?

Return to 293.

195.

TO LOOK FOR WHAT? A WEAPON?! ARE YOU INSINUATING MY DAUGHTER WOULD HAVE KILLED A GOOD WOMAN?

You've offended Mordecai Cushing. Leave to 289 before he uses his weapon.

196.

REALLY... YOU HAVE NOTHING BETTER TO DO THAN TO ASK ME TO WRITE MY OWN NAME?

THERE. I HOPE YOU'RE HAPPY.

ANYTHING ELSE I CAN HELP YOU WITH?

Jonathan Brighton

Return to 181.

197.

Wrong! If you have any attempts left, go to 294. Otherwise, go to 53. You may not return to Emil Jackson.

198.

Noted by Sherlock Holmes: The Duke's dagger seemed dirty and dusty. That means...

That he doesn't take care of it. 168

That it's not his. 98

That it couldn't be the murder weapon. 204

199.

I DON'T KNOW WHAT YOU'RE INSINUATING, BUT I *CAN* SEE YOU SUSPECT ME OF SOMETHING...

The gravedigger is offended and is now giving you the silent treatment. Return to 246, but ask him no further questions.

200.

I CAN'T TELL YOU WHETHER IT'S *CLAIRVOYANCE* OR A MIXTURE OF OBSERVATION AND DEDUCTION. THE FACT IS HER PREDICTIONS WERE VERY OFTEN RELEVANT.

Return to 68.

201.

COME IN, COME IN!

I KNOW WHY YOU'RE HERE.

I WILL TRY TO BE AS ACCURATE AS POSSIBLE.

AFTER MONTHS OF EXCAVATION, I FINALLY LAID MY HAND ON THE TOMB OF KING PARKHOUMET IV AND HIS RENOWNED TREASURE: THE GOLDEN SCARAB!

I ASSURED ITS TRANSPORT TO LONDON, FOLLOWING ALL SECURITY PROTOCOLS. I CAN GUARANTEE YOU THAT I DELIVERED THE SCARAB TO THE CURATOR.

I COULD HAVE LEFT SHORTLY AFTER THE RELIC WAS SAFELY DELIVERED. BUT... I QUITE LIKE THE MUSEUM'S STAFF, SO I STAYED A WHILE.

I WAS IN THE OFFICE WITH MISS FORRESTER, TEACHING HER HOW TO MAKE ORIGAMI CHICKENS.

SHE WAS WORKING ON HER THIRD ONE WHEN THE CURATOR CALLED HER AWAY TO HELP WITH THE WINDOWS, AS A STORM WAS APPROACHING.

I WENT DOWNSTAIRS A FEW SECONDS LATER. WHEN I PASSED BY, THE CASE WAS INTACT.

I WAS SEVERAL ROOMS AWAY WHEN I HEARD SOMETHING BREAK!

I WENT AS QUICK AS I COULD. WHEN I ARRIVED, EVERYONE WAS ALREADY THERE, WE WERE ALL RELIEVED THE SCARAB WAS THERE, TOO. BUT THEN I NOTICED IT WASN'T THE THE REAL SCARAB.

WE'D LIKE TO ASK YOU A FEW QUESTIONS.

Ask your questions of Miss Forbes at 306.

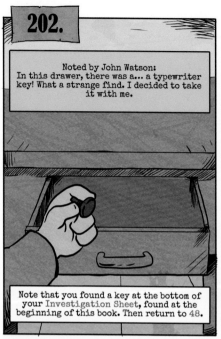

202.

Noted by John Watson:
In this drawer, there was a... a typewriter key! What a strange find. I decided to take it with me.

Note that you found a key at the bottom of your Investigation Sheet, found at the beginning of this book. Then return to 48.

203.

AS YOU NOTICED, MR. WALTER ISN'T HERE TODAY, BUT I WILL SHOW YOU TO HIS ROOM.

187

204.

Noted by Sherlock Holmes:
That's it! If the dagger was dirty, it's because no one has bothered to clean it. And if it were the murder weapon, it would also have traces of blood on it.

Return to 93.

205.

And another thing... the footprints are larger (you estimate size 12) and seem deeper than those left by the bare feet.

Watson can ask Holmes for advice at 233.

Holmes can use his powers of deduction at 12.

206.

I'M SORRY. THAT FACE DOESN'T LOOK FAMILIAR.

Return to 297.

207.

You notice a fingerprint on the scarab.

Go to 224.

208.

NEAR THE MUSEUM'S ENTRANCE. NOT FAR FROM EMIL'S POST.

Return to 61.

209.

GENTLEMEN...

If this is the first time you've been to see Miss Forbes, go to 201. Otherwise, go to 306.

Ask your questions of Mordecai Cushing at 116.

220.

Wrong! If you have any attempts left, go to 294. Otherwise, go to 53, You may not return to Emil Jackson.

221.

VERY WELL! EVERYONE IS SO LOVELY! ESPECIALLY, THE LITTLE SECURITY GUARD. I LIKE HIM QUITE A LOT!

Return to 306.

222.

THERE'S A VAGABOND THAT HANGS AROUND IN THE WOODS: MR. NORWOOD, THE NEW GRAVEDIGGER.

AND THERE'S THE GOLD DIGGER.

OH REALLY?

Return to 293.

223.

I COULDN'T REALLY SAY, FOR SURE. A LOT, I WOULD IMAGINE...

Return to 61.

YOU... ARE YOU POLICE, TOO?

AM I IN TROUBLE?

DON'T WORRY. WE'RE HERE TO HELP. DO YOU REMEMBER YOUR NAME?

I... NO... SOMETIMES IT FEELS LIKE IT'S COMING BACK TO ME, THEN IT DISAPPEARS JUST AS QUICK. THEY CALL ME JOHN DOE AROUND HERE.

I DON'T KNOW WHO I AM OR WHERE I'M FROM. I DON'T KNOW... ANYTHING.

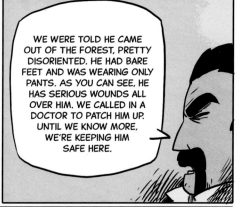

WE WERE TOLD HE CAME OUT OF THE FOREST, PRETTY DISORIENTED. HE HAD BARE FEET AND WAS WEARING ONLY PANTS. AS YOU CAN SEE, HE HAS SERIOUS WOUNDS ALL OVER HIM. WE CALLED IN A DOCTOR TO PATCH HIM UP. UNTIL WE KNOW MORE, WE'RE KEEPING HIM SAFE HERE.

COULD WE ASK YOU A FEW QUESTIONS? PERHAPS THEY'LL HELP JOG YOUR MEMORY...

Ask your questions at 297.

226.

SIZE 12, WHY?

Return to 153.

227.

Inspector Bradstreet agrees to get fingerprints from the suspects to compare against.

However, it's going to take time. Go on and question them all in the meantime. As a reminder, their names can be found at 245. Come back here when you're ready.

Have you visited all four suspects? Go to 287.

228.

YES. BUT I'VE FOUGHT HARD TO MAKE A NAME FOR MYSELF IN THIS PROFESSION. AND I DON'T THINK I DID TOO BADLY, AT THAT.

Return to 306.

229.

Something was buried here, and someone dug it up with a shovel.

234

230.

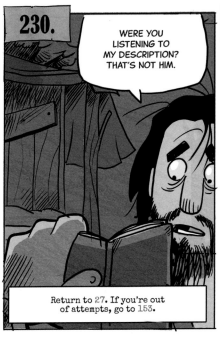

WERE YOU LISTENING TO MY DESCRIPTION? THAT'S NOT HIM.

Return to 27. If you're out of attempts, go to 153.

231.

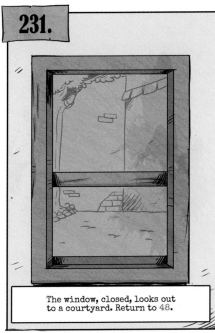

The window, closed, looks out to a courtyard. Return to 48.

232.

You can barely make out what's inside.

86

233.

IT'S ELEMENTARY, MY DEAR WATSON. THE PERSON WEARING SHOES WAS CARRYING OUR AMNESIAC.

THEIR FOOTPRINTS ARE DEEPER, BECAUSE CARRYING SOMEONE MADE THEM HEAVIER. THEN THEY LEFT HIM ON THE GROUND. JOHN DOE WOKE UP AND WALKED UNTIL HE FOUND CIVILIZATION. FROM THERE, OUR SUSPECT WALKED INTO THE BRUSH, WHICH IS WHY WE DON'T SEE ANY TRACKS HEADING THE OTHER WAY.

Return to 247.

234.

This is where the map leads, no question. But it seems like someone got here before us.

When you're finished here, go to 58.

235.

You notice that Husk is covered in hair from his cats.

One thing this certain, he couldn't have touched anything without leaving a trace of cat hair behind. Return to 128.

236.

That is undeniably the hammer used to break the case. You note that there are no fingerprints on its handle.

↓ **75**

If you have the GREEN DOCUMENT, you can:

ask Holmes for advice at 101 if you are Watson.

use your powers of deduction at 45 if you are Holmes.

237.

WAIT, NO! I... I PROMISE YOU THAT I... I'M NOT...

You've frightened him! Return to 297, but ask him no further questions

238.

WHY WOULD THIS PLACE BE WORSE THAN ANYWHERE ELSE? WE'LL LIVE WHEREVER WE PLEASE!

You've angered the Frobishers. Return to 293, but ask them no further questions.

239.

NO, THAT'S NOT THE PERSON I SAW.

Return to 27. If you're out of attempts, go to 153.

240.

YEAH, THAT'S HIM ALRIGHT! HE LEFT THE CEMETERY CARRYING THE AMNESIAC ON HIS BACK.

Bravo! From now on, you can find this portrait in your LEATHER NOTEBOOK. Go to 153.

241.

You estimate the shoe size to be about 12.

242.

Well done. You solved that puzzle brilliantly! Make note of these typewriter keys on your Investigation Sheet.

Then return to 4.

243.

I BELIEVE IT BELONGS TO SARAH ANN. IT'S ONE OF HER ARCHAEOLOGICAL TOOLS.

Return to 61.

If you are Watson, you may ask four questions, but only three if you are Holmes. For each question asked, mark the corresponding checkbox (with a pencil). Be careful, as certain questions could offend your witness, and cause them to refuse to answer further questions.

☐ Do you know the man in the photo? 51

☐ Who lives around the woods? 18

☐ Is there anything special in that forest? 106

☐ What is your shoe size? 264

☐ Do you have keys to the cemetery shed? 165

☐ Have you ever locked anyone in? 199

☐ If you have it, show him the GREY PAPER. 123

☐ If you have it, show him the LEATHER NOTEBOOK. 13.

When you're finished, go to 58. You can come back later.

Clearly, something happened here! The barefoot footprints end here, only to continue... as shoe prints over there?!

15

205

248. You notice that there's no fingerprint on the case.

249.

THAT RESEMBLES HIM, BUT THAT'S NOT QUITE IT.

Return to 27. If you've used all your attempts, go to 153.

250.

Nope! If you have any tries left, go to 294. Otherwise, go to 53. You may not return to Emil Jackson.

251.

Noted by John Watson: That's it! There must have been two windows outward facing windows open.

You have have everything you need to solve this case. Go to 33.

252.

YES, THAT'S IT! THE CLIENT USED A FAKE NAME, BUT IF HE BELIEVES IN MADAME YVETTE'S NUMEROLOGY METHODS, HIS REAL NAME WILL HAVE THE SAME NUMBER OF LETTERS AS JEREMIAH WOODHOPE.

It's up to you to find it in the index at 170.

253.

Gravedigger's Shed

G. Norwood

86

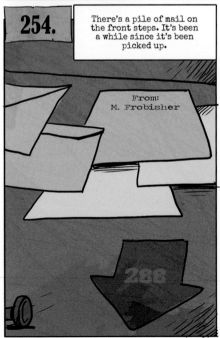

254.

There's a pile of mail on the front steps. It's been a while since it's been picked up.

From: M. Frobisher

288

255.

313

You notice that the box has no prints on it.

256.

HOLMES... CORRECT ME IF I'M WRONG, BUT ISN'T THIS THE MANOR OF THE DUKE OF SHIRE, BENEDICT BRIGHTON?

EXACTLY RIGHT, WATSON.

AH, HMM... HELLO, GENTLEMEN.

THAT WAS FAST, I DIDN'T EVEN RING THE BELL.

AH, THAT'S MY BUTLER, JOHN WALTER. HE'S HEADED OUT. I'VE GIVEN HIM THE DAY OFF.

MR. DUKE, SIR. I'M--

SHERLOCK HOLMES. I RECOGNIZE YOU.

NEEDLESS TO SAY, I KNOW WHY YOU'RE HERE...

POOR MADAME YVETTE.

COME IN.

I'LL TELL YOU EVERYTHING.

146

257.

Noted by Sherlock Holmes: Hmm, no. A serrated blade couldn't have left a cut so thin and clean. That's not it.

Return to 172. You may not use your powers of deduction any further on this subject.

258.

Noted by John Watson: Hmm, no.... Mrs. Hudson spoke of two noises right after another, almost instantaneous. No one is fast enough to do that.

No more hints! Go solve the case at 33.

259.

More size 12 fooprints!

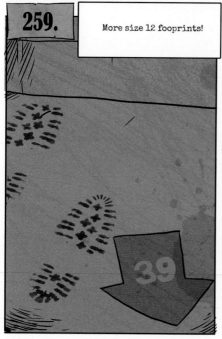

260.

WE NEVER GO DOWN THAT WAY!

Return to 293.

261. These ropes had been cut, although there's nothing in the room that could have been used to do so.

157

262.

I HIGHLY VALUE THE REPUTATION OF MY FAMILY. ALAS, JONATHAN DOES NOT KEEP THE COMPANY OF... VERY GOOD PEOPLE.

Return to 93.

263. The Duke leaves to fetch his son. A young man with a serious look returns. He looks to be about 20 years old. 181

264.

WHAT A FUNNY QUESTION! I WEAR A SIZE 12 SHOE.

Return to 246.

265.

THERE'S MR. AND MRS. FROBISHER, THE RETIREES. THERE'S THE OLD GOLD DIGGER. AH, AND THERE'S A NEW GRAVEDIGGER AT THE CEMETERY, BUT I'VE NEVER MET HIM. OH, AND ME!

Return to 153.

266.

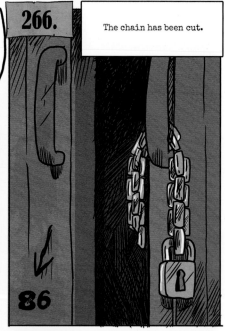

The chain has been cut.

86

267.

MY FATHER WOULD DO ANYTHING TO PRESERVE THIS FAMILY'S HONOR.

Return to 181.

268.

VERY WELL WITH SARAH ANN AND EMIL. BUT WITH MR. ATKINSON, IT'S MORE... LET'S SAY HE CAN BE A LITTLE TYRANNICAL TOWARDS ME.

Return to 61.

269.

Noted by John Watson: No. Decidedly, I was thinking too much like a doctor and less like a detective.

No more time to investigate!

Go solve the cas at 33.

270.

DR. WATSON, YOU'VE COME TO HELP ME? UMM... ALL ALONE?

ALRIGHT, IT'S BETTER THAN NOTHING.

It's Mrs. Hudson, your landlord. Go to 67.

271.

OH YES! IT'S MY JOB. PLUS, I'M THE ONE WHO FOUND IT, SO IT'S SORT OF MY BABY!

Return to 306.

272.

273.

Being a doctor, John Watson can examine victims and bodies. The wound Mrs. Hudson suffered is long, thin, and fairly straight. What do you think could've left a mark like this?

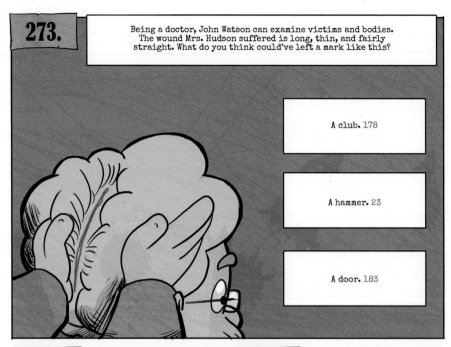

A club. 178

A hammer. 23

A door. 183

274.

I CAN'T REALLY SAY SHE HAD ANY ENEMIES. ON THE OTHER HAND, MANY FOLKS TRUSTED HER, AND CONFIDED IN HER THEIR DEEPEST SECRETS. THAT MAKES HER A LITTLE DANGEROUS, I SUPPOSE.

Return to 68.

275.

HERE? NOTHING BUT PEACE AND QUIET! AND I CAN TELL YOU THAT WE HAVE NO PLAN OF LEAVING ANYTIME SOON.

Return to 293.

280.

AFTER HER GRUESOME PREDICTION, I WAS SO LOST IN THOUGHT THAT I DIDN'T NOTICE WHETHER THERE WAS ANYONE THERE OR NOT. SORRY.

Return to 93.

281.

I WAS SEEING SOMEONE... BUT... I STOPPED.

Return to 181.

282.

You notice a strange inscription on the wall. Those are ... James Moriarty's initials! He has left you an extra puzzle to solve. But don't worry if you can't figure it out. It has no impact on your investigations.

284.

It's the moment of truth! Add the results of the four cases from your Investigation Sheet.

All done? Go to 210.

285.

I HIGHLY VALUE MY FAMILY'S REPUTATION! IMAGINE IF PEOPLE KNEW I WAS VISITING A FORTUNE TELLER... YOU CAN UNDERSTAND WHY I WOULD OCCASIONALLY ASK MY BUTLER TO GO INSTEAD OF ME.

Return to 93.

286.

YES?

If you have the GREEN DOCUMENT, go to 227. Otherwise, return to 75.

287.

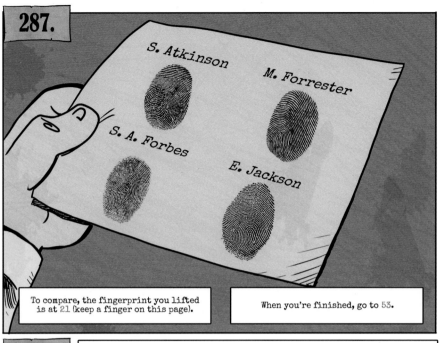

S. Atkinson

M. Forrester

S. A. Forbes

E. Jackson

To compare, the fingerprint you lifted is at 21 (keep a finger on this page).

When you're finished, go to 53.

288.

You have come here to investigate "The Amnesiac of Highgate Woods". If this is not true, return to the index at 170.

When you're finished, return to 58.

289.

What would you like to do now?

Return to the scene of the crime. 172

Consult the index. 170

I'm done investigating. I'm ready to solve the case. 37

290.

Does this symbol remind you of anything?

4

291.

You notice that the Duke's dagger is on his belt...

JB

You ask to examine it at 126.

292.

Rats! If you have any attempts left, go to 294. Otherwise, go to 53, and you may not return to Emil Jackson.

293.

If you are Watson, you may ask four questions, but only three if you are Holmes. For each question asked, mark the corresponding checkbox (with a pencil). Be careful, as certain questions could offend your witnesses and cause them to refuse to answer further questions.

☐ Do you know the man in this photo? 64

☐ Have you been to the cemetery? 260

☐ What are your shoe sizes? 212

☐ Is there anyone special in the woods? 275

☐ Who else lives around here? 222

If you have it, show them the GREY PAPER. 73

☐ Why do you two live here, in particular? 238

If you have it, show them the BROWN NOTEBOOK 194.

When you're finished, go to 58. You may return later on.

294.

You lost him. The streets here are a veritable labyrinth! Thankfully, there's a map.

90

220

197 · 292

250

56

HEY, I SAW HIM! FROM HERE, HE WENT STRAIGHT AHEAD, THEN HE TOOK THE FIRST RIGHT, THEN THE FIRST LEFT! AND AFTER, HE TOOK THE FIRST RIGHT!

THE TROUBLE IS, I DON'T KNOW WHERE WE ARE ON THAT THERE MAP...

Watson has two attempts, Holmes only has one. If you're unable to find him, go to 53. You may not return to Emil Jackson.

295.

THE REGISTRATIONS ARE ALL OVER THE PLACE. SO WE CAN'T COUNT ON THE BOTTOM NAME BEING THE LAST CLIENT TO HAVE BEEN HERE.

REMEMBER: THE PEOPLE WHO WROTE THEIR NAMES HERE TRULY BELIEVE THAT THE NUMBER OF LETTERS IN THEIR FIRST AND LAST NAME WOULD PROVIDE SOME INDICATION OF THEIR FUTURE.

Return to 117.

296.

AH HA! HERE ARE THE FINGERPRINTS OF ALL THE SUSPECTS.

287

297.

If you are Watson, you may ask four questions, but only three if you are Holmes. For each question asked, mark the corresponding checkbox (with a pencil). Be careful, as certain questions could offend your witness and cause him to refuse to answer further questions.

☐ Did you have any identification in your pants? 308

☐ What is the last thing you remember? 141

☐ Is there someone we should contact to let them know you are ok? 169

☐ Did you know that lying to the police about being an amnesiac is a crime? 237

☐ What is your shoe size? 214

☐ How did you receive those wounds? 192

Watson can examine his wounds at 59.

Holmes can use his powers of deduction at 100.

If you have it, show him the GREY PAPER. 193

If you have it, show him the BROWN NOTEBOOK. 206.

When you're finished:

If this is the first time you've questioned the amnesiac, go to 283. Otherwise, go to 58.

298.

299.

You have come here to investigate "The Lifeline". If this is not true, return to the index at 170.

WHAT ARE YOU SAYING?

MADAME YVETTE IS DEAD? YES, YES... I... I KNEW HER.

COME IN AT 180.

300.

John Doe's footprints. He doesn't have very big feet. Size 9, at most.

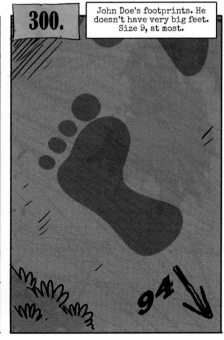

301.

THAT'S NOT IT! THE CLOCK IS STILL TICKING!

If you have any attempts left, return to 210. Otherwise, go to 35.

302.

SOMEONE STOLE IT FROM ME.

Return to 181.

303.

Noted by Sherlock Holmes:

No... something was escaping me, but I couldn't put my finger on it.

Return to the scene of the crime at 172 or to the index 170.

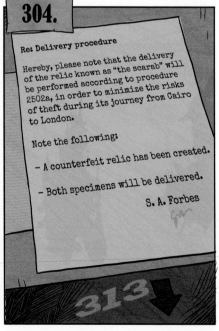

304.

Re: Delivery procedure

Hereby, please note that the delivery of the relic known as "the scarab" will be performed according to procedure 2502a, in order to minimize the risks of theft during its journey from Cairo to London.

Note the following:

– A counterfeit relic has been created.

– Both specimens will be delivered.

S. A. Forbes

313

305.

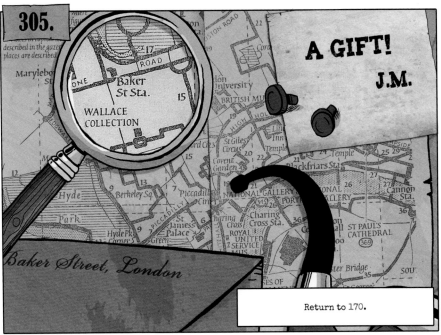

A GIFT!

J.M.

Baker Street, London

Return to 170.

306.

If you are Watson, you may ask four questions; and only three if you are Holmes. For each question asked, mark the corresponding checkbox (with a pencil). Be careful, as certain questions could offend your witness and cause her to refuse to answer further questions.

☐ Would you be able to distinguish real vs. fake by looking at them? 271

☐ Where did the fake come from? 52

☐ Was it your hammer that was used? 211

☐ How do you get along with the team? 221

☐ Archaeology, that's a difficult career, no? 228

☐ How much would a relic like that sell for? 316

☐ If you've found it, show her the PINK ENVELOPE. 312

☐ When you're finished, go to 53. You may return.

AND WHERE ARE THE PEOPLE WHO WERE PRESENT DURING THE THEFT?

THE THREE EMPLOYEES HAVE BEEN TAKEN TO THEIR HOMES, WITH OFFICERS GUARDING THE EXITS. NO ONE IS ABLE TO LEAVE THEIR HOUSE OR HAVE ANY GUESTS.

THE MUSEUM'S CURATOR IS STILL HERE, HE HASN'T MOVED.

I'LL TAKE YOU TO THE EXHIBITION HALL.

GENTLEMEN, RIGHT THIS WAY.

75

312.

OH, EMIL SEEMS TO
BE WITH SOMEONE. TOO
BAD, I LIKED HIM.

Return to 306.

313.

77

304

255

314.

No one here! Jackson has escaped!

315.

COME IN!

If it's your first time visiting Maud Forrester, go to 36. Otherwise, go to 61.

316.

IT WOULD CERTAINLY BE TOUGH TO SELL. YOU WOULD HAVE TO KNOW PEOPLE IN THE ART MARKET...

...BUT IF THE THIEF FOUND A BUYER, THEY COULD DISAPPEAR AND NOT HAVE TO WORRY ABOUT MONEY FOR THE REST OF THEIR LIFE.

Return to 306.

Count how many typewriter keys you found.

If you have fewer than 20, you have 1 attempt to enter the correct number.

If you have between 20 and 29, you have 2 attempts.

If you have between 30 and 39, you have 3 attempts.

If you have 40 or more, you have 4 attempts.

Go to 284.

319.

BRAVO, HOLMES. YOU MADE IT OUT!

YOU WON'T BE SO LUCKY NEXT TIME.

AND WHAT IF WE JUST FINISH IT NOW?

I KNEW VERY WELL THAT YOU WOULD FIND THE PERFECT VIEW FROM WHICH TO ADMIRE YOUR WORK, AND THAT FROM HERE, YOU WOULDN'T BE ABLE TO SEE ME LEAVE THROUGH THE INNER COURTYARD.

?!

GO ON, YOU KNOW HOW GRACIOUS I'VE BEEN. YOU WERE ENTERTAINED. AND I EVEN LEFT YOU A WAY TO GET YOURSELF OUT OF IT. YOU YOURSELF WEREN'T QUITE SO FAIR BACK AT REICHENBACH FALLS!

MORIARTY!

NO!

NOT THIS TIME!

YOU'RE NOT GETTING OFF THAT EASY!

Noted by Sherlock Holmes:

It was over, for now. I wasn't about to let him use death as an escape, whether real or simulated. His macabre game of investigations would end here. Later, after delivering him to Lestrade, I asked Watson not to record this sinister story in his chronicles.

I preferred to remember Professor James Moriarty as an elegant criminal genius, not as a madman, eager for vengeance.

Go to 320.

YOU'VE COMPLETED THIS ADVENTURE, BRAVO! I'VE HAD THE OPPORTUNITY TO LOOK OVER THESE CASES AGAIN, AND I'VE ARRIVED AT THE DEFINITIVE SOLUTIONS. THEY CAN BE FOUND ON THE FOLLOWING PAGES.

I'LL EXPLAIN, ACCORDING TO MY DEDUCTIONS, HOW CERTAIN EVENTS CAME TO PASS. THIS MAY INCLUDE REFERENCES TO CLUES I FOUND THAT YOU MAY HAVE MISSED.

HOWEVER, IF YOU HAVEN'T COMPLETED THE FOUR INVESTIGATIONS, I ADVISE YOU NOT TO LOOK AT THES PAGES YET. YOU'LL SPOIL THE EXPERIENCE OF INVESTIGATING FOR YOURSELF.

IF YOU DIDN'T FIND THE RIGHT CODE ON THE FIRST TRY, IT'S BECAUSE ONE OF YOUR ANSWERS WAS WRONG.

I ENCOURAGE YOU TO BEGIN YOUR INVESTIGATIONS ANEW, PAYING CLOSER ATTENTION TO THE DETAILS. YOU CAN EVEN CHANGE WHETHER YOU USE ME OR JOHN.

THE SOLUTIONS FOR THE FOUR INVESTIGATIONS CAN BE FOUND:

- IN 321 FOR "THE CAT OF BAKER STREET"
- IN 322 FOR "THE LIFELINE"
- IN 323 FOR "THE AMNESIAC OF HIGHGATE WOODS"
- IN 324 FOR "THE SCARAB OF THE BRITISH MUSEUM"

WHEN YOU'RE FINISHED CONSULTING THESE SOLUTIONS, YOU CAN CONTINUE TO THE END OF THE BOOK, WHERE A SCORING SHEET AWAITS YOU.

Notebook of Solutions

Do not read before
you have finished
all four
investigations!

321.

THIS *CASE* WAS THE SIMPLEST OF THE FOUR, BUT HAD ITS FAIR SHARE OF REVELATIONS.

The first is that Mrs. Hudson also owns the neighboring building, 219.

Like every day, she went to the caretaker's suite, passing by the apartment she was planning to rent, and that she assumed was still vacant.

With her back to the hall, she began to refill Rosalie's bowls.

Rosalie, as usual, took the opportunity to stretch her legs in the hallway. But this time, the apartment across the hall wasn't deserted after all. Intrigued by the noise, the aforementioned tenant opened the door to see what was going on.

And finally, Duke Benedict Brighton.

Being concerned about his reputation, he used a fake name. As he believed in Madame Yvette's numerological methods, his pseudonym possessed the same number of letters as his first and last name.

Thanks to a handkerchief, Lord Brighton discovered a connection between his son and a girl from a poor family, the famous Esther Cushing.

The boy had offered it to her, but the cloth had been sent back to the manor.

The Duke asked his son and Esther not to see each other anymore, even though she was pregnant.

When Lord Brighton signed the numerology notebook that day, he received a shock!

Esther Cushing's name appeared among her list of clients.

He could only assume that Madame Yvette knew the Cushing girl's secrets, but couldn't bear the thought of them being repeated! The risk was too great. It would be a scandal! Brighton made a decision...

He waited for Madame Yvette to read his palm...

...and grabbed hold of her hand, immobilizing her.

He explained what he had to do and she begged him not to, promsing that she wouldn't say anything to anyone.

But Brighton wasn't listening. He proceeded to slide his dagger in the fortune teller's side, using his left hand.

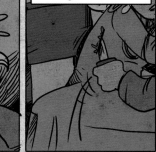

He escaped by the side door, his blade dripping with blood.

He cleaned his dagger with his son's handkerchief, which he had on him, and threw it in the trash.

Then he walked out to the street, as if nothing had happened.

When Julie, Madame Yvette's assistant finally worked up the courage to go see her...

...it was too late. Madame Yvette was no more.

Lord Brighton learned that we were on the case. So he gave his butler, John Walter, the day off.

He thought that his clean dagger would seem suspicious. So he hid it in his butler's room...

... and replaced it with a dirtier blade belonging to his son Jonathan.

Perhaps you noticed that the dagger's initials...

...weren't quite right.

As further proof, you could have noticed that Jonathan Brighton's writing, although similar (as may be the case between father and son, was not the same as the writing found in the numerology notebook.

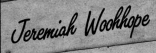

Jeremiah Woohhope

Jonathan Brighton

Also, Lord Brighton was the only left-handed suspect.

THE CORRECT ANSWER WAS THEREFORE DUKE BENEDICT BRIGHTON, NUMBER 26.

HE'S SINCE BEEN ROUNDED UP AND PUT BEHIND BARS.

It's hard to say what gave way first:
John Doe's strength, or his spirit.

Frobisher had the map and knew
how to read it. And John Doe
ended up losing his memory from
the beating he endured.

Frobisher abandoned his
prisoner and the map
in the shed...

...and left to dig up the treasure.

I think he acted alone, without
informing his wife. In fact, there's
no trace of her footprints – size 7 –
anywhere...

Furthermore, the correspondence from
the railroad (train tickets to flee the
area, perhaps?) were addressed only to
Morris Frobisher.

The new gravedigger, Garrett Norwood, found John Doe tied up in the shed.

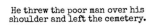

He threw the poor man over his shoulder and left the cemetery.

Martin Norris, a vagabond who didn't yet know Norwood, saw them walking by.

The gravedigger abandoned John Doe close by. The amnesiac had been tortured in HIS shed, and he wanted to avoid any problems with the law.

He disappeared into the forest, leaving the poor man to wake up all alone.

BUT HOW CAN WE BE SURE THE GRAVEDIGGER DIDN'T TRICK US? OR THAT WE WEREN'T FOOLED INTO BELIEVING THAT THE GOLD DIGGER HAD LEFT LONG AGO?

There were absolutely no footprints near the gold digger's cabin, and his tools seemed to have gone unused for quite a long time.

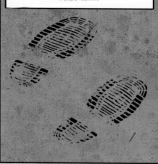

What's more, even though the footprints we found near the treasure site were a size 12...

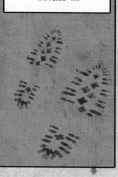

...they didn't match those of John Doe's "savior"...

...nor those that led to Garrett Norwood's residence.

THE PERSON RESPONSIBLE FOR OUR AMNESIAC'S CONDITION WAS THEREFORE MORRIS FROBISHER, NUMBER 62.

AGENT GREGSON FOUND AND ARRESTED HIM TRYING TO CATCH A TRAIN HEADED OUT OF TOWN.

324.

When she arrived upstairs, she noticed that her desk drawer was open...

... and, to her horror, found the scarab! She had no idea that it was the counterfeit.

To avoid getting into any trouble, she simply placed the scarab back in its case. This is why there were fingerprints on it. Then, the others arrived and Miss Forbes informed everyone that this was not the real scarab.

HOW *CAN* YOU BE SURE THAT THE *CURATOR* WAS THE THIEF? WHY NOT THE SECURITY GUARD OR THE ARCHAEOLOGIST?

By process of elimination! At the time of the "robbery", Miss Forrester was giving an origami chicken to Emil, which he put in his booth.

It was the only moment she could have done it.

Plus there were the fingerprints, or rather, the lack thereof.

No prints on the box in Miss Forrester's desk, yet there were some on the scarab itself.

A strange inconsistency.

And there were no fingerprints on Miss Forbes' hammer either.

And the only one wearing gloves was Sagamore Atkinson...

His plan worked perfectly. He was going to get rich by selling the scarab on the black market, and his assistant (whom he hated) was going to be take the fall.

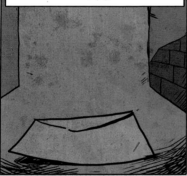

Perhaps you found the love letter Miss Forrester wrote to Emil, the security guard...

If you then went to see her, you would have seen that Emil was ready to take the fall for her, believing we were setting a trap for his beloved.

BUT WORRY NOT! EMIL WAS RELEASED, AND ATKINSON WAS ARRESTED. AFTER SEVERAL HOURS, HE CONFESSED TO THE THEFT, AND HANDED OVER THE RELIC.

THE *CORRECT* ANSWER WAS THEREFORE "THE *CURATOR*", NUMBER 23.

Scoring

Score 3 points for each mystery solved using Watson.
Score 4 points for each mystery solved using Holmes.

The typewriter keys:
If you found between 10 and 19, score 1 point.
If you found between 20 and 29, score 2 points.
If you found between 30 and 39, score 3 points.
If you found 40 or more, score 4 points.

If you defused the bomb on the first try, score 1 point.

Out of the 20 possible points, how many did you get?

If you scored fewer than 10, you are a mediocre detective, but you can improve by playing other "Sherlock Holmes" Graphic Novel Adventures.

If you scored between 10 and 15, you are a good detective. Continue your training to progress towards excellence.

If you scored between 16 and 20, you are an excellent detective! Congratulations!

Enjoy this adventure? Find more great games like this at: VanRyderGames.com

Based on the characters created by Sir Arthur Conan Doyle.